Jane Jolly and Robert Ingpen

TEA AND SUGAR CHRISTMAS

NLA PUBLISHING

Tea

Kathleen peered into the sugar jar. Her face tightened. There wasn't a single grain left. She would have to go without until Thursday.

'Where's the tea?' called Dad.

'There's none left,' said Mum. 'You'll have to wait until Thursday.'

Kathleen smiled at Dad. 'You'd better buy a bigger packet next time.'

'We'll stock up on everything,' winked Dad. 'Especially things for Christmas.'

The Tea and Sugar Train only came once a week on a Thursday. But the special Christmas train only came once a year.

Today was Sunday.

Four more days without sugar.

Four more days until the Christmas train. Please, please be on time. Please don't be late.

Kathleen couldn't wait. She ran outside and scrambled up the hill-face at the back of the house. She held her breath and listened. Only a cicada answered. Cricka. Cricka. Cricka.

The next few days dragged. The heat rolled in from the desert and hung heavily, entering the house at every door and window crack.

There was no school on Thursday and in the afternoon Kathleen climbed the stony hill-face again. She sat staring out across the empty desert.

The air was still and breathless. A droplet of sweat rolled down her face. It tasted salty as it hit her mouth.

In the distance she could see the glistening railway tracks heading into the siding. She listened intently. Was that the tinkle of silvery bells? She squinted. She could see a light. Yes, there it was again, making its way through the saltbush. It was coming! Ever so slowly the train clacked along the tracks towards town.

PROVISION STORE

Kathleen slid down the hill and ran through the drowsy town. She burst inside.

'It's coming! It's coming!' she shouted.

Dad looked up and his eyes danced a jig.

'Now, what might be coming, girlio?'

'You know, Dad. Come on. Let's go.'

'At last, more tea and sugar,' said Mum, from the end of a paper chain.

Kathleen grabbed the wheelbarrow and started running with it. Her feet pounded the hot track, searing like scones on a griddle. She could hear the screeching of the train as it pulled into the siding. As she ran, others emerged from their tin castles, cheering and calling out across the shimmering landscape.

PROVISION STORE
FLOUR

WELFARE CAR

When she reached the siding Kathleen stopped. The smell of hot oil and metal filled the air. Her mouth was parched and her new dress hung limply, damp with sweat. Dad and Mum caught up and stood in the shade of a drooping peppercorn tree. A Christmas tree, which had been decorated by the children on the line, stood wilting in the heat.

Clinks and clunks filled their ears as the train drew to a stop. Guards jumped up and down from carriages, looking important.

Everyone waited. A crow cawed, long and languid. Ark, ark, aaaaark. It flew to a telegraph pole and watched.

Kathleen left the wheelbarrow and edged forward. Her eyes widened. The guard sauntered along the track. Kathleen held her breath. He reached up and pulled on the carriage door.

At first it stuck and Kathleen let her breath go with a sigh. Then he pulled hard and it opened.

C R

BUTCHER

Kathleen screamed with delight as she saw him.

Father Christmas.

His beard was blinding. His clothes were so Christmas red! Just like all the pictures she had ever seen of him. And here he was. Real. Here, in the middle of her desert.

The guards pushed a set of steps in front of the carriage. One by one eager children climbed them and told Father Christmas their wishes. Clutching their presents, they were carefully lifted back down.

It was Kathleen's turn. She had waited for this moment for so long. She had dreamt of it. And now she stood before him. Her heart drummed against her chest.

CPR

Father Christmas's eyes crinkled and smiled. 'And what would you like for Christmas, little girl?' he chuckled. Kathleen tried to speak. She stared into his eyes.

'There must be something you'd like,' he urged.

She licked her lips and whispered, 'A present. Please.' His loud 'Ho, Ho, Ho' made her jump. Father Christmas placed a parcel in her hand. 'Merry Christmas, little girl!' As Dad lifted her down, her eyes didn't leave the big, bright man in red.

Kathleen sat in the shade and carefully opened the package. She squealed when she saw the book. Her eyes didn't leave the pages as she flicked excitedly through it.

When the shopping was done, the carriage doors shut with a clang. The train blew its harsh whistle. The crow let out a long, dry croak and flapped away. Kathleen stood next to the track, clutching her book, and sighed. It was all over. She watched as the train pulled slowly away. Metal on metal. It screeched out of town. Through the saltbush and past a lonely bent acacia, it disappeared into the distance.

At home Mum put the kettle on for a cuppa. Dad waved the packet of tea. Kathleen looked for the sugar. There was nothing. In all the excitement they had forgotten to buy the sugar.

'No worries,' said Dad. 'It's Christmas!' and he picked Kathleen up and spun her around the kitchen.

FLOU
TEA

CR
PRICE LIST

There were no shops or services in these settlements. The train carried everything they needed—household goods, groceries, fruit and vegetables, a butcher's van, banking facilities and at one time even a theatrette car for showing films. Once a month, a priest travelled on the train to minister to his flock, presiding over weddings, baptisms and funerals. In the late 1970s, medical services provided by Flinders Medical Centre were included. A nursing sister and assistant were always available, while medical officers and dentists periodically made trips.

Those waiting for the train could see it coming for miles. Men shaved and women put on their best dresses and a dab of make-up to greet it. Imagine their excitement when the train finally arrived.

Families pre-ordered special requirements and these were made up and packed into the Provisions van. There were no supermarket trolleys for these shoppers though. Shopping was taken home in wheelbarrows!

Mrs Harris likes a chat while waiting for her sausages.

Tommy can't wait to get his hands on those biscuits.

Old Bluey thinks there are some dog treats in that wheelbarrow

TEA AND SUGAR TRAIN

For 81 years, from 1915 to 1996, the Tea and Sugar Train travelled from Port Augusta to Kalgoorlie once a week. Also known as the slow mixed goods train No. 5205, it serviced the settlements along the Nullarbor Plain, a 1050-mile-long rail link. It was a lifeline. Not only did it bring much needed supplies, it brought news of the world—by way of newspapers and books—to the isolated workers and their families. The train crew also brought news from down the line of births, marriages, divorces and deaths.

After World War II many single post-war migrants came to Australia from all over Europe. Many of these men ended up as fettlers (maintenance workers) and gangers (in charge of a group of labourers) on the East–West line. They often lived in basic railway camps or galvanised iron houses in the small settlements along the line. Aboriginal and Afghan workers also played an important part in the construction and upkeep of the line.

That's it for this week. Hope we haven't forgotten anything.

Fresh meat was ordered weekly. Livestock was carried in the butcher's section that included a slaughter van. As the train approached a siding, the meat order was checked and the butcher selected a beast. By the time the train stopped it had been slaughtered, gutted, skinned and sectioned into the cuts ordered. In 1982, the Butcher van was dropped in favour of pre-packaged meat.

In the Community Welfare car, babies were weighed and given check-ups, children were vaccinated and adults consulted the nurse. It was simply a matter of queuing up at the car and waiting your turn. There were often magazines—donated by the citizens of Port Augusta—for the women to catch up on the latest celebrity gossip. In later years, the Welfare car included a dental clinic and toy library.

The Provision car carried all the necessities: from laundry items to baby products, pet food to women's nylons and of course tea and sugar! However, chocolate could only be carried in winter because of the torrid heat in summer which melted it.

Hurry up, train!

The best day of the year.

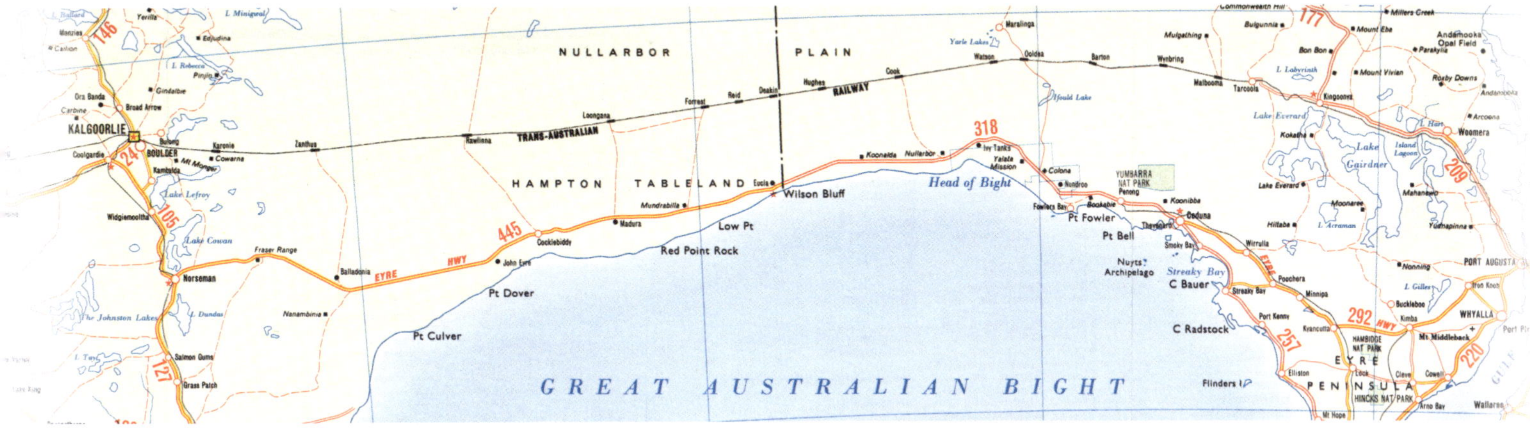

The Bank car served as paymaster to the workers and often doubled as a post office.

The biggest excitement for the children was the first Thursday of December every year, when Father Christmas travelled the line. He distributed gifts to all the children on the way, including those of railway workers, those in isolated communities, and station kids. No child missed out.

For 36 years, Alf Harris worked as a locomotive inspector and was a very close friend of Father Christmas. His wife, Nancy Harris, described it as 'the joy of his life'. Children would often dress in their best clothes to meet Father Christmas and every child left with cool drinks, lollies, comics and a present.

A lack of water along the Nullarbor meant that the last of the steam engines ran in the 1950s. They were replaced by diesel engines, which didn't need to stop for water and coal.

With the introduction of concrete sleepers there wasn't the need for their replacement and upkeep. Gradually the already tiny settlements grew smaller until some disappeared altogether. The last Tea and Sugar Train ran on 30 August 1996.

Our favourite food from the Provision store.

Published by National Library of Australia Publishing
Canberra ACT 2600

Reprinted 2015 (three times), 2018, paperback version 2022, reprinted 2025

ISBN: 978-1-922-50740-2

The National Library of Australia acknowledges Australia's First Nations Peoples—the First Australians—as the Traditional Owners and Custodians of this land and gives respect to the Elders—past and present—and through them to all Australian Aboriginal and Torres Strait Islander people.

Commissioning Publisher: Susan Hall
Editor: Irma Gold
Designer: Amy Cullen
Image coordinator: Jemma Posch
Research assistance: Bob Parker
Production coordinator: Melissa Bush

Printed in China through Asia Pacific Offset.

Find out more about NLA Publishing at library.gov.au/discover/nla-publishing.

A catalogue record for this book is available from the National Library of Australia.

List of National Library of Australia illustrations (p 32–35):

If you are interested in trains, you could also look at the National Library's Buckland collection which has images relating to all aspects of Australian railway history. http://nla.gov.au/nla.pic-an11434053

Keith Fellowes
A Resident of Karonie Buys Meat in the Butcher's Car of the Tea and Sugar Train on the Trans Australia Railway 1960s
b&w photograph; 9 x 9 cm
Pictures Collection
nla.pic-vn4589311
Courtesy Australian News and Information Bureau

Don Edwards
The Storeman on the Tea and Sugar Train, Sam Main Talks with Customers in the Provision Store, 24 June 1974
b&w photograph; 15 x 19.5 cm
Pictures Collection
nla.pic-vn4589269
Courtesy Australian Information Service

Keith Fellowes
A Resident of Coonana Sets off for Home with a Wheelbarrow Load of Supplies from the Tea and Sugar Train on the Trans Australia Railway, May 1968
b&w photograph; 9 x 9 cm
Pictures Collection
nla.pic-vn4589294
Courtesy Australian News and Information Bureau

Keith Fellowes
Residents of Coonana Check Their Purchases beside the Provision Store Carriages of the Tea and Sugar Train on the Trans Australia Railway 1968
b&w photograph; 9 x 9 cm
Pictures Collection
nla.pic-vn4589292
Courtesy Australian News and Information Bureau

Cliff Bottomley
The Trans-Australian Railway Line of 1108 Miles from Kalgoorlie (Western Australia) to Port Pirie (South Australia) Includes 297 Miles without a Curve –the Longest Straight Stretch of Track in the World 1960
b&w photograph; 16.3 x 21.6 cm
Pictures Collection
nla.pic-vn3513402
Courtesy Australian News and Information Bureau

Trans-Australian Railway
Port Augusta Station 1917
sepia-toned postcard; 7.6 x 12.7 cm
Pictures Collection
nla.pic-vn3098712

David Dare Parker (b. 1958)
Alf Harris the Tea and Sugar Santa and Local Children Walking along the Railway Tracks, Forrest, Western Australia 1989
colour photograph; 21 x 29.6 cm
Pictures Collection
nla.pic-vn3544606

Shell Guide to Australia (detail) c. 1970
map; 72 x 82 cm
Maps Collection
nla.map-vn2293351-s1

Advertisments left to right:
Advertisement for Weet-Bix
page 47 in *The Australian Women's Weekly*, 4 February 1950
http://trove.nla.gov.au/ndp/del/page/4312808

Advertisement for Bushells tea
page 52 in *The Australian Women's Weekly*, 4 February 1950
http://trove.nla.gov.au/ndp/del/page/4312813

Chas Shiers
Buy Australian Fruit 1930s
colour poster; 73 x 48 cm
Pictures Collection
nla.pic-vn5056565

Blotter advertising Billy Tea
in *Collection of Australian Blotters*
Ephemera Collection
nla.aus-vn3308163-8-2

Blotter advertising McAlpin's Flour
in *Collection of Australian Blotters*
Ephemera Collection
nla.aus-vn3308163-14